Afterbody

First published in 2025 by Blue Diode Press
30 Lochend Road
Leith
Edinburgh EH6 8BS
www.bluediode.co.uk

ISBN: 978-1-915108-28-9

Typesetting: Rob A. Mackenzie
text in Pilgrim LT Roman

Cover art: Divya Singh
Cover design and typography: Rob A. Mackenzie

Diode logo design: Sam and Ian Alexander.

Printed and bound by Imprint Digital, Exeter, UK.
https://digital.imprint.co.uk

Afterbody

Medha Singh

BLUE DIODE PRESS
EDINBURGH

for my mother
for my sister

"...I understand, all right. The hopeless dream of being—not seeming, but being. At every waking moment, alert. The gulf between what you are with others and what you are alone. The vertigo and the constant hunger to be exposed, to be seen through, perhaps even wiped out. Every inflection and every gesture a lie, every smile a grimace. Suicide? No, too vulgar. But you can refuse to move, refuse to talk, so that you don't have to lie."—Ingmar Bergman (from 'Persona', 1966)

Contents

Δ

∞

Δ

∞

Δ

After

I held you under open heat
  by a river that warmed and curved
   in the distance. It swirled beneath trains
    in that strange society. Our dawns tapered,
     turning gelatinous within the deep grammar
      of love. I peppered these quiet words for you, across
       the marmalade dusk, and now you stand in a field, within
        my solitude. There is a God moving her dark hand in water over the straits
         where whales go to calve. In shallows they find muster for the new babe.
        The grass glitters, daisies quiver in their windy groove as you begin
       to remember our time: I couldn't gather you up, knowing
      your nose, your tongue might find another, snug
     in the air coiling our concrete past. It now cracks
    around the waists of women you think you
   finally learnt to love. Think of me
  as a hand in the pines, from a purer
time, as error and ghost, still coring
 your chest: stubborn,
  unmoving.

Another Life

I'm writing love on a napkin
as mourners gather on a mound
for the disgraced dead, still
in grave-clothes underfoot—
suddenly, slow pianos   sing
in air, the shifting earth
moving its cadavers to an ache
in the ocean. Here they are, the wretched
reborn as willows, contorted into pains
they don't recognize. Bad men become trees.
The earth forgives them, as do I. They begin
to give. The wicked also dream
of love. They know darkness overhead
means night before and night behind, yet drops
of starlight have shot through earth's evening;
overhead, gingkoes have flared
against sun. Evening over tarmac, evening
beneath lorries, where dogs huddle
for warmth, and for miles on end
the quiet noise of town. At the end
of the last mile, me, pouring this syrup
on a napkin. Things I can't say yet:
Oh, pianos. Oh, love. How we begin
to open   under black water.

Lunch, Boat

The church on distant ground, its cross like a spinning top—
the kitchen at the restaurant ripe with hot butter sizzling
through fresh ramsons. A staghorn knife quartered the afternoon.
At the table on the prow, gleaming fish lay inside crushed ice—
such liquid music before the food's arrival, swish and slosh,
birthed in water. *Such textures* sitting in the narrowing light,
our chests taut with fear—political views, fissured and chivvied,
don't speak to me of values: how they take time to marinate, cook.

What we mistook for love, really just refractions through feeling.
It was over then. Borrowed light mirrored in droplets at once
prism and sphere. In their sheen I saw reflections of lost friends,
the same lumens darting through the two of us that once blighted
Saturn, its petroleum oceans, and lay on the granular snouts of foals
tethered to a cart, in a sunlit field.

Touch

How do I turn back from all these hands have touched?
In another world, you'd want it to be silk, mead, ice sheets, dust—
I'd say yes, yes to it all yet touch the black wind inside your ribcage
instead. It was then I learnt of a cold thing. We've gone on making
something of invisible sorrows in the night, as with elements:
sitting on a potting wheel, the dance and congress of ocean limb,
orphaned earth, stray wind and old fires. It's dark inside an earthen pot,
so the water cools in summer heat. I now know this bright chill—
ingots of gold, driftwood in winter and old rubber tyres in snow
that burn the village dead. I have known all one could touch: tribal
song on another side of the forest. I knew by the way
it held me first. I walked away, still having had these hands
on the newness of the strange—cobblestones, new waters,
                    this rain.

Look at the bronze bird between white birches—

                    moonwashed and soft, now the oak
above the rocks, and the woman sitting
inside the window with her cat.
Sometimes this makes up for what she, drunk
on an old pain, mistakes for the present.
The sounds of the day roll up like canvas
as points of starlight slide through
the grape-black sky. There emerges the voice
again, leaves whirling in idle wind, always
singing a tune she knows—how foolish
was Eve, never saw that Adam was
her father. Adam did not know how to touch
a woman. She thinks of herself
as a pale star whose days are flashing
through the bare trees. She is inside the ocean,
wending her way through water. She is bone
-tired, kissed dry. She is alluvium and foam,
she's taking tonight's train, running away
from home. Falling asleep in a shivering seat,
she wakes to morning, baking her face
under baltic sun. Senescent, how she floats,
            now chewing on the ashes of God.

Edinburgh, Spring

The clouds now burn off
under white light, bracken and bramble
    browning in white weather. Pink blossoms
trail in translucent air, I sneeze
        constantly.

    Here, in The Meadows, yet another
creature, lovely yet ill-favoured,
  struggling, appeasing volatile men,
    frozen in time   until she is finally
too leathered to matter. You see,
    she's foreign

        too, dribbling like a train, surprised
always at the imbecile he's made of her.   Her face now calm
    in a bid to justify her cotton
dungarees in this joke of a summer. Watch her
    try   to contain fidget, shiver and retort. Watch
her go on   of home with nostalgia and dread.

Now becoming still as barbecue smoke
rises from soil, petals suspending in air
        as the sun goes on breathing
the moisture out of this earth, she looks around
        and feels their rub redden her eyes.
All the open skin across the field, she sees the pollen
fall on dimpling muscles, shirtless bodies as they grow
pink, laughing   around the ritual fires.

Birds—greenfinch, blackbird, carrion, corncrake
pollen rolling in odd syncopations,
        time is but sound.

It's early,
    too early for capoeira and dancing
but the light will begin to purple as a clot on my thigh,
    the men will soon sashay in, heavy

with septum piercings, to teach the unloved
    how to dance with fire.

I am quiet in what is left of this light, slightly
    euphoric as I see on the left here, a child
sleeping on his father's stomach
        who sleeps inside the stomach
 of a hammock, lulled
    by the warmth of body and day.

The Meadows

The slow tension of your step I know
so well, now this absence in air, where
your body moved next to mine. I drop
my eyes, they shine under white sun.
In the red world behind closed eyelids,
I fall inside a river of lavender carrying on
into our days as we lie in The Meadows,
kissing. God's feints startle the rising moon,
they come for me as you leave, my cheeks
saline now that it's clear the sun eats
only so much darkness, the dark sick
of itself, a mendicant praying for light—
I alone enter the black cave of your mouth,
coil its stone tongue with mine.

Painting Our Time

(for the mothers in Kashmir)

1.

Stretch a canvas across the pane of reality
and you'll see all that's surviving. See the curving earth
in a fist of smog, see Amazonia sprouting smoke
from its feral, mad belly. Miscarrying, she is borne
by the arrogation of fetid soldier breath—

A sculptor uses her fine chisel of gunmetal
and contrition, gnawing, picking out bullets
from holes in ribcages where hearts keened:
a pellet gun, an aerial camera found these bodies
scattered across the valley.

A girl ravaged in the temple, a boy blinded in a classroom
by the incalculable torpor of men in saffron, of men in green;
it's hard to see them inside the clangour of ritual bells, beneath
the rustle and shag of trees, behind the bushes, they lurk.
At home, a door ajar, clearly kicked in—
there is mother's yellow dupatta draped over,
put the crud in the grave with all the pellets,
the bullets and mallets always drawing
our eyes to the sea.

Elsewhere, across the quaver of human ears
in a forgotten country, mothers
are anxious against the tightening noose
of their days, furtive, telling their sons time
is shortening and aloft, the light
closing, that it will all pass.

2.

Say 'amor fati', say 'we will never foresee
the nature of things that draw us into their love.'
Say, 'the wish, the hope, the dream, the ephemeral
sole embrace, the dry tug of it all', say
'the story is never over', nothing is ever over,
say, 'the sun in the sunflower seed is the veil
of denial rent open', say, 'the end of hope
now gives way to clarity', say, 'in the end, you stood
upon the rocks at Sahastradhara', say, 'they told you
water cuts stone, all the gorges and great reefs
don't stand alone', say 'in the wide swathes of time,
everything will wash over us', say 'we live on
as the taste of brine in a whale's mouth',
say 'We?...', 'We will be washed away.'

3.

(for Rohith Vemula)

Hammer in the canvas over the frame
Hammer in your dreams upon the canvas
Hammer the truth into popular mindlessness
and watch the world baulk at it like a dalit forced into birth.
Forced into a name, into living, pummeled to death.

4.

Are you waiting for the winter to wane into an upright fog?
    Are you waiting to align your spine with its quiet dignity?

Are you waiting for the man and woman living
    in your belly   to fall in love?

Are you wishing for them to converse eternally?
  Do you want to stop being, because being is not-doing and not-
doing is the undoing of being?

Are you waiting for your embarrassments to wither
   into a convenient forgetting? Are you afraid they won't?
     Are you waiting for the simpletons who never understood
        you enough to forgive you? Are you?

     Are you waiting for desire to learn it's shy of the mark? Are you
       waiting for the day you'll finally know the words, won't fall short?

    Do you wish these words did not exist in such excess?
      and has lexical excess been the undoing of your charm?

    Do you wait for the hour when others will cease
   to skirt around the bush? And push the detritus
   of their peccadilloes   into the universe?

                Do you covet your
                neighbour's ox? Your best
                friend's wife?

    Did you know your days were nothing, when you couldn't
    control   the destiny of your words.

5.

Grief never belonged to one, always a guest.
Watch mother hold the flag at half mast
her eyes welling as she casts my fathers bones
into the ceramic waters
of the Ganges. Her husband swimming away into the after.
An empty beehive still sways, hangs
on the porch of her home in the village.

6.

Praise the farmer that unburdens
the land of his own weight.

Praise the children who wish he had
not hanged himself, taken poison instead.
Praise

the village that knows poverty
as pestilence. Praise, praise the woman
who forgives him.

Rewilding

Ecstasy, I was told
is to lie outside oneself
  the way we think of gardens
being the only way the earth shakes
  awake from its taupe dream and enters
world into verdure, or the way invisible
  things become apparent in visible things,
the wind undulates in wheat,
  light flickers along stones under running water.
Now, look at the life with bones and words, small
  but heavy sad, with all its fine writing
by the refined, consummate and dead.
  All I want in the anxiety and aimlessness
of world and ecstasy is the courage of gardens
  that endure the quiver of time. The kind
that could make me stand through
  the cremation of a child in snow, where
there is none to attend,
  but a blanket flowing along my spine.

Inconsolable, I'm inconsolable.

∞

Delhi, Day

Travelling by moonlight into morning
I cast a smokeless fog over winter.
Southward, on the damp body of this map
there, the fishermen have begun throwing
their nets that clutch the slow & bulbous sea—
Northwards, this easy winter light between
the nodes, as it guards the stones therein
that built a city by a thousand touches, all
her mausoleums. Now the clouds clear, clear
into blue, a blue on heaven's dome.

Delhi, Night

Congeries of impossibility—
imagine a love up there,
a vortex hotting up.
Warmth, arriving
in the quiet cold.
Temple bells muting
their clangour,
the glass factory done
slowly blinding
its rubber slippered workers,
the Muezzin too
is squarely asleep.
A dog doused in the moonlight
is swatting flies, in the orange glare
with its mud-robed paw.

The Lesson

I recall my late father's palms over the flame, the stove rounding at the edges. All through the white afternoon the light curled at the farthest air; his hands checked for temperature before he plonked the fish over fire, assessing the heat or warming his hands against the biting cold; the moment I knew that to write or draw was prompted by taste, smell, or touch. Emotions writhed in the chest and throat and back and gut, much before language became a preoccupation, or I encountered the word 'affect' in a friend's mouth in college, a word too big for him even now.

In early youth what is the world but a defibrillator of your theories? To be proven wrong, was to sense the taste of your food change, feel the air turn dense with guilt—the beginning of conscience. Something tastes a certain way, only to learn it doesn't. If I stick my nimble fingers in the socket and turn the switch on, I'm likely to find out it's a one-time experiment. I was lucky to survive it at the time.

I wondered what happened to the goat before it was all shanks&ribs + aroma&spice in our kitchen. My father left no stone unturned when I released at him a volley of childish questions (well, I was a child); the era began when all my theories were finally to fail. The imagination lived, yet struggled without material grounding, without a fulsome vocabulary. I struggled. Speech wasn't enough. It was time to go to the butcher. Father took me.

Of all things I did make projections for, I did not for once hypothesize how a market smells, I already knew its intimate odors: rot, chiefly. This is the truth—simulacra of fresh vegetables and some fraying and fermenting, discarded on the street, blaring vehicle horns, the din of chaos; rickshaw pullers hollering at pedestrians, a flower seller at the exit gate of my residential complex, comfortably perched on a chair, next to a small bonfire, absorbed in his Hindi newspaper, acrylic muffler wrapped around his head and ears (wool an exclusively middle class accoutrement), prostitutes in saris waiting for sundown as they waited for the policemen to start either soliciting or harassing them—the bravest of local gamblers.

A short distance off, vendors: oranges nervous with open pores; glistening, smooth apples in gradient hues of red, yellow and green; mounds of bananas of varying quality and price; variegated textures on the leaves cradling the cauliflower, the wild cabbage, the plump tomato, curly tailed turnips and slender radishes, the green-pimpled bitter gourd, depressed aubergines, sweet potatoes, okra, the commonplace lauki, tinda, and parwal. A clear geometry visible in each sight, every sample of what was borne by this earth for us. Children teetered, tethered to their mothers jonesing for a bargain, to feed their husbands in a few hours, some feared beatings in failing to do so. I saw a gash and a wound, a blue mark on a woman, and another, and another. Proud of this quick deduction, I was full of my own senses, without conscientiously acknowledging that beatings were more the norm than the exception among the poor; although they did their messages with the middle classes (in whose homes the violence was of a different kind, but not by much, I knew because my father thrashed me time and again). These, the inhabitants.

Streaming in and out of that infinite stretch, this wide, whole street that contained itself as it hyper imposed into that strange and invisible lattice of time and space. Everything mid-confluence, all was electric. Peopling now with the laughter of schoolchildren in rapid, autonomous trajectories.

What did I not know? All that I was to learn in the five years that followed. This is an Indian metropolis. It gathers abundance, and speaks of affluence. While all affluence ever meant was our propensity to waste, that is not what we had and needed but what indeed was made waste. Our desire for excess, as farmers in villages far and near mixed poison in their mortar and pestle where there was once turmeric, ginger, onion, garlic, clove, cumin, coriander—ready to die, as they could no longer pay their loans, gift saris to their wives, feed their children. I knew this because my mother wrote a poem about this happening first hand. There was something morbid and remote about this *mandi*, and its sense of total self-containment. It stood erect, chin up, like a vain man acutely alert to his own beauty, chronically aware of the rarity of such a thing, and to go on womanising—no chore at all. This strange vanity evinced in the debris, of all that was not bought at the end of the evening. The carts overturned on the street and the produce left there for the homeless to pluck from; but mostly, it became foetid waste the next day, filling up the chalky, dry wind of the winter with warm, sulphuric odours. The bright, hot air in the summer. Thus was this city once.

...and is the story of every metropolis: go back in time and always a lingering myth supporting its theory of origins. Beyond that, only darkness, a forest, the great rocks. The animals? Chimaeras, dragons, gargoyles, gremlins and ghosts, and not a being named that could defeat us in that ancient game of kill-or-be-killed. We had no names for them, really; only a semblance of the term 'monster'. *Raakshas, vetaal, pishaach.*

History moved with my feet, as my hand rested in my father's. We continued on, father gracefully walking towards our destination, me tottering along. We arrived at the butcher's, still holding my father's hand, watching that little thing desperate and flailing, overpowered by the enormous palms of a man in white: fine, cottony Kurta-Pyjama, spotted with animal blood all over him, slowly morphing into a muddy brown. My father said, 'blood does not change colour on silk' as though he knew exactly what I was to go home and do: paint the scene, as one does. 'That's why so many Chinese paintings are on silk, they've survived a long time.'

The butcher came in and proceeded to mount the goat. Releasing it from its harness made of braided coconut husk, he grasped it by the horns and ears in a tight grip, lay one leg over its back, and the other left to hang over to the other side, until he was standing over the animal as if in a game of hopscotch. The goat bleated away in misery, its legs squirming in uncertainty, the creature's eyes pursing shut, a hint of a tear at the corner of one eye—it knew. The butcher's hands pulled its head backwards and then pushed it down as one does when you're trying to murder a screaming woman by drowning her in a bath. I heard the bone snap.

The second butcher ran in strong with an axe and in one quick, imperial stroke, severed it; its head fell to the ground. Small, short lived fountains of blood sprayed on and then, after a warped moment, turned into weak spurts until they stopped. My breath quickening, I wanted to say something, but wasn't quite sure what.

Consciousness does not leave the body immediately once hacked: a severed head, I think, lives for at least a second before its light leaves the cranium. This half body was something one could not waste. One *simply* couldn't. A scene such as this with chickens had earlier turned my little sister into a vegetarian, and she remained so well into the future, until she was eighteen; it had a very different effect on me. I came to believe, years later, with this incident in mind, that packaged meat was the coward's route. He who chose not to witness the violence, is not able to hunt the animal for himself, did not have a right to the prey. Though this wasn't as well articulated at the time, I felt it intuitively. I watched him suffer, and let him die. I couldn't bring the beast back, so what was left? To honour its life and not waste a fibre on its bones. I, then, resumed to look on as the goat was methodically sheared, skinned, eviscerated, in fact turned over and drained of blood, hacked into clean cuts, and stuffed into two polythene bags that were black as night, and then handed over to my father. As the help mopped the blood off the floor, the room thickened with a ferrous odour. We left.

Our journey back was sombre, we said not a word to each other. I didn't hold his hand this time, I think. I wanted to understand why he led me to such a scene, why was I to witness this? What kind of man was he, after all? There is a rehearsed and learned detachment about Rajput men when it comes to violence, I'd observed as I grew up. Clans of rulers, and warriors were in a state of constant battle without break throughout history, it had been so for centuries, before the great force of the Mughals defeated us in the battles of Khanwa, and then at Haldighati. It's strange to think their origins could be traced to Genghis Khan: *Mughal, Mongol,* I toyed with these words when we, two sisters, learnt of our family's origins, as we grew up eating all the food they brought to the north: kebabs, butter chicken, bhuna ghosht, raan, nihari, haleem, all that needed us to first breed, suborn then decimate these creatures. To think, now, we live in times when a man is lynched in broad daylight on the suspicion of carrying beef, that he's a muslim, so he must resign himself to secondary existence in his homeland. I think it cruel, objectively cruel in the western context to consume meat as it is: packaged and cleaned of the reality of its availability, the way they are clinically bred, forcefully kept, tortured in dark rooms until they reach the grinder. If you have any ethics, you'd avoid it, yes. Then it gets complicated here at home: my solidarity lies with the muslims. It's in their lesson that we have our lesson. The prophet lived in the desert where nothing grew. They have given us this city, its food, its ruins, an entire history, clothing, architecture. This wild city-within-a-city is the crown prize, though we pride ourselves most on our cuisine here.

What is Delhi now but 'a capital in search of a country'? I'd read that phrase in a book I found poorly written, or perhaps it wasn't, and I just did not really take to the social sciences because of their clinical, austere language. There was no blood, no juice to suck from it.

I'd learn about my father's tendency towards violence years later, tethered to his Rajput ancestry, both of which contribute to such strange parenting decisions. That would explain why I was still being thrashed, a decade later. That he'd force us to see the violence for a reason: when my teenage sister would weep, a few years in the future, the sweet child, over her dead goldfish, and my father would cast them out on the balcony for the crows to pick on.

'Ask him why he did that, sister, go on', I'd said to myself. She would, of course. He would turn around to say 'we go where we came from: back to the soil.'

Δ

Aerie: Vignettes, Delhi

Mvt. I

Furrowing sound over the balcony, birdsong
 and regret, the breeze with its fine toes
 in the Asoka trees
     emerging from the northern pines—
weeks through years sliced by its whistle. I toy, tongue
a pomelo I pick from the fruit seller's cart under mizzle,
monsoon
   he kisses the minarets that flicker
in my eyes. My eyes, always running westward
as they tumble
into fog that roils over tombs, sun still
beating down on red rock and rain, soft prick
of water on a boy's arm, look—
doves begin flying against the sound
of schoolchildren who now circle
the sundial
by the busy highway.

Midday susurration of trees in easy winter light. I am, again. Slow
    to wake within the folds of a hoary December
afternoon, from a dream like a blurred negative of a lost world

    a time   where a kiss once lingered in the moment,
was summoned at will, I can *be* in it.   Children soaped by women,
lovers feeding them dates without worrying over the waltz—a deficiency,
all this crock about our love being deeper, and its need grander
    as we fall through the seasons to the welter   of our lives.
To grow unfit for social smiles,
    to find   the world teetering along, growing eternally jejune,
yet not anymore
    than ourselves.
To scoff at guileless youth.
    To move   onward, yet never move
on.

Memory.   Blurring against shadow.   Against shadow.   Against silence.

Bodies wake, squally creatures thrashing in time's fishing net.
What has grown   will never grow again. Kelp and horse
by the river. We marvel at the miracles among these noisy plains—the rustle
of twisting trees, stretching outward in the mustard light. I say to the dog
stretching in prayer with its forelegs in offering   and to the gloaming,
                                                            here I stand
with an egg and an egg, feeding one mouth so feeding all, I ascend.

I stand on a tower, Yamuna swelling through traffic, verdure, concrete and
                                                            fear—
    separating heat from wind, breath from parking lots.
Goodbye, I say; she waves, and throbs. I make tracks. Cut through fern,
gaze across motorways   for signs of life. I, arriving at cafes
and tombs with infinite names in a place with many: Hastinapur, Indraprastha
Dehlvi, Dilli.   Your arms, eyes, your body   they become
 home and habitat, trading in a thousand
    histories and tongues.

A cricket match.
The fear of death is not the fear of death
but of a certain loss of pleasure, a certain threat
to the page.

Pause. Breathe. Fall through August rain. Age.

Whispers—whispers echoing in the deep, marrowless halls of this skeleton.
Whispers ushering current through narrow alleyways / stirring whistles advance
and violet shadows rush within the hollow bones
of macilent boys   that throng with the great slap
of palm against palm and thwack
of leather ball against hard bat. Torrents: a heatwave upon another,
breaking against the unrelenting resolve
of young men pregnant with dreams of supereminence.

Noble, preternaturally masculine, rippling spirits as flags on high.
Shoulders with bones, chests with bones, the hollows of their eyes.
They've stretched the afternoons of my years long.
No one, ever, seems to win the game.

Feather. Swivels slow, to the ground
off the sunny terrace

all the way down,
hurtles on in its menace of a life

on this easy, quiet town
no floating, neither zigzag nor
wide curl

drops, drops straight, crowns
downward, whorls a hole in the thick air,

opening a centre of gravity
that wasn't there. Entering

life's machinery, determined
to enter its fate at your feet

(where the sun has drowned)
firmly, without a sound.

Wake
from a Rabelaisian dream
    and search in the dark
for his luminous forehead, find his bright
    tongue with yours, he's sweating
in his sleep, he's half asleep. Casting his spindly,
    broad chassis, he mirrors
the rhythm of your breath, your dancing shoulders—
    he finds the music for the moment. The sonata collapses
as the dream. You're left on your back, finger drawing
    circles over his spine as he lies adjacent, breathing
on his stomach. The sea glittering against the shore
    of this world, somewhere else
it is flinging light on our dry faces; it is the sea,
    bright, green tinted glass, floating upon itself.
Breaks, the day. Breaks, the breeze. Breaks, your discipline.
You're late   for everything.

Begin, begin the noise again, the fleeting, dangling, falling rain
the hobbling dog, the homeless god, throwing a foot forward and afar
a language slain. Bit by bit, they've made the trek: once they were all
tall men, having beaten speed backwards and found the extinct sparrow,
excavated the story of this city's beginning. She had no extremities,
no outer limits,
only the sound
of the scratch
on the door
the scratch on the window, only the most frightening scratch
on the window, as the last man on earth found himself alone again
in this fog, on this green, round jade, the wind that bid adieu. Adieu, it whistled.
Said, *come in*.

The moon beams infinite blades of light into the night over a street stampede—
hungry mouths and bare feet, our own grand exodus
of every Everyman parting the city. They've walked from villages
with scabs on their soles yowling for their lands. Children are crossing forests
to get home,
they're chewed up by beasts and maggots on the trail.
See, how things changed so quickly, quickly, only to change back
to their old colour, to things with no colour
things already and forever reconfiguring—white rose withering
to a cold brown, a red one to a thing paper-thin, purpling—
it stains a souvenir, a napkin. While the bottlebrush looms overhead
to be shed in February, the silviculture sleeps by the Church, the Gurudwara,
that feed and fed this aeon's wretches till the last sigh, how the bottlebrush
hangs about us, over us now: a falling omen.

They stand, here they stand, unfit and a tad too sensitive to peachy sundowns:
dog and god, homeless together day after day, beneath starless, smoggy nights,
but for the subtle call of the great, white speckle: Venus masquerading as the
north star.
Here they are, asking, why are you here, half-breathing, half-beating heart?

Mvt. 2

Hot tears, hot clouds, hot earth.
Lambent sun, grasping all. Eagles exiting dead trees
beneath sharp rain: they go   wet, heavy, slow

perch on quiet ground, warm mud clasping
their talons, sienna light lining their beaks.

When it doesn't
rain, wingèd and bright, they hang
from heaven   stretching out, they enter
that last darkness
that mirrors Vesuvian clouds—
they sink beneath the tree-line,
into a lower earth, where the sun drowns.

The night, now still
as a dark tower.

Between fingers of crops made of clean air, the great
Himalayan rift.   Time was adrift   seething

in darkening
treetops that swayed   as they cooled

slapped by the torque of frigid winds,
evergreens once warmed by evening
where the sun had bled.

I was once pure ethanol   my chest beginning
to ignite as I entered atrium   after atrium,
living room, bedroom

paid cabbies of yore, hoping   for the perfect party.
Time was adrift, wild, in pale light.

Coral, cochineal grief,
   grief, in waves
     renewing
       into new
behemoths

'Abate', a grumble in the skull. 'Quiet, please. Smile.'

As stillborn children, one after the other, voices
  voices came with a resolve
    to punish
     us for the past

their half souls circled these eyes, I walked
through Delhi's smoke, wept
by her gutters   rank, under rain.

until I was all fire, all sphere, made of light,
my planets   orbited this heat
as it grew from the ground
in wayward mizzle, monsoon
called me / calling me, still;
as though I had an answer
to the lack of surprise, at anything at all,
the bereaved tended to carry.

My palm is still reaching for you in the dark,
    across the density, to find you asleep–
I grasp your neck, the small of your back
    to touch   the electric chill of gold
Look, now, how we dance, move
from grief
    to ecstasy.

Mirror, scour some truth under the rim
of my moist eye,   beneath the olive
epidermis, something sacred,
sparkling, sombre has lurked

I have been reading
the words

wear great learning
lightly.

The passage into the streets
of thought
    is through a kind of becoming—
an arrow races through a cellar window:
    to be quick, charming, and leap
towards one (without doubt)
    except I'm a hawk, not an arrow
gutting the sky
    not the cobalt against the gold
not the Athene owlet drinking
    from the pail
under a feral, quiet moon
    not the man in the linen suit
by the burning
    bougainvilleas

    holding a smile for me
despite himself
Against the cool, singular shadow of night
    I lie on the bed and notice a flash of light
wash the ceiling
    and know that a car has whizzed past
forty feet below:
    the truth has arrived quietly on this earth
to take some of us away

What I'd give
    to be loved
                as I once loved

With your feet, take your turn, quietly
    in the waving fern; collapse

in its embrace, hear in your secret ear, the music

of lovers segue
    out of each other's bodies
  as they part.

Each morning, the sun-man commands his chariot
                        ambles into my bed
by night, he climbs   into the leaves,
    is gone

thrive, Medha, in the cold centre
    of your sopping, open gash.

Illness, a dream, a Stygian guard—
the boatman wading towards me, soft spoken,
well-mannered
'imperially slim', calls himself Utnapishtim

Here, a eucalyptus tree, quickly filling
up with parrots beside it, a dead
sentinel with white branches

stands, sheared
by time, a lone hawk at its summit.

Frame of fire, bone. Mirror of blood,
stone: umbra of sundials
followed me through aeons, now
collapsing   into the long hand,
perch   &   tick, quiet

on this sweet wrist.

                                        Kiss it. Long.

Time is a thick drift that drags all

what the drift drags

spills into the eye

Mvt 3.

Curtain of water over a soft face
by the hand pump, the red mug
dives into the iron pail—she's drawing
out viscous residue and working
up a lather. Few pleasures on earth
as sweet and private, as running
one's hands through loose tornadoes
of human hair. Shadows
of flying barbets passing over her face.
Northwards, we see them rise against the road.
In the warm car, the sitar twirls, our ankles are free.
　　Look, how cold and elegant:
a mountain, its wooded feet.

Atop a mighty rock: you flatten your hand perpendicular
 to your forehead, kill the sun, displace
 the eagle, seated in your aerie
 a view symphonic: no colour to speak of here, no waves cresting against the shore,
     no precipice to ponder upon, no infinite-charcoal depth to fling
our shame. We're organs, writhing, daydreaming the hours away
     under glinting raincoats. Anxiety widening to boredom over the hours
 memory's flower

 pollinating the smoke, a world of pullulating markets
 axed by heat.

   Abandoned concrete mixers, half old bulldozers on the barren street / sit quietly
in post hail moisture, gathering rust. And the light is tea clear, lemon brown, forest
     emerald.
We move in centuries with ease between these gales, this world of pages—

   Let your eyelids drop, the wind crack against them, give ear to the ancient
                                                                        destriers
flailing with their fervent neighs in war, the red billed lapwing on the civil servant's
     painted porch crying for India's independence, layering the despondent breath
of this great blood-raw crack of land, and land crinkling up against the Radcliffe
                                                                              line.
   Regard the morose hound
by the businessman's verandah, all the bees of the world lapping up sorrows
     discarded by our Gods and lawyers, consigning them flower to flower / at a time.
Watch as they splay out on alabaster against tarmac. History against truth.
     Remarkable heat, white light draping the city
it always did / through every geriatric impulse
     of famished, defeated kings.
I cling to it all, I release it (and exhale). This pain
     was never mine.

A line is the edge of a shadow,
A body lingers as an expression of life. The shadow   is not the object.
The body needn't live. The body is a shadow of the life in it.

रेखा। परछाई। शरीर। अंत।

Serpent Eagle traverses the skies, faltering.
Unable to map the total dimensions
of this world, she glides injured, a hole through
her left wing, she's fanning it out. Doubt, pain, ignominy.
Watch her move, clap the air; I imagine the grit
of her cousins, when injured seasonally,
tearing out their nails, perched atop the same tree
for months, umoving, unloved
until total renewal—ready for the jubilee, to sink,
finally, freely, again into the earth's depths.

She who sweeps up the nameless,
the homeless, the parched, the dead
off the streets, every year in this chimeric city,
the annual heatwave claiming their blood, grabbing
their souls in its maw—what is her name?
Designation? Dante's guide. Beatrice?

No, not Virgil: the lover.
There he is, flowing between alleys—
London, or Delhi. His back is turned to me, he's toying
with an old pocket watch. When I first looked at him, I saw
the nervous gaze you do on young men's faces. Then
something else: my face, it reminds him of all
the women that make them run: Man's soul, always
out of time.

Head bent now, he faces
his pocket watch, looks
up and walks into the mouth
of a dark wind.

Once Esther and I decided to leave Delhi, its fear
cloaked in arrogance had begun to hurt.

We ate crayfish which they told us was lobster at the Bombay
Gymkhana Club. Then, we went to Kochi and found a doll's head
on the beach after we grabbed some live blue crabs in the market.
It reminded me of an abortion. At Alleppey, on a boat, I saw a
Cormorant for the first time drying its wings as it spread them out.
We descended on dry ground and watched the ropemakers weave
coconut husks into long ropes and I learnt the skill to a passable
degree. I saw the cormorant the whole while sitting with a wide
wingspan for an hour, it was perched on a stick stuck to the mud
beneath the water. An astrologer told us we were going to be friends
forever and have the same number of children. It was no coincidence
we met.

Ext. Stage Left.

Railride,
          to the south seas:

Sun changing character country to country, de Chirico's long shadows.
               I burned the fields with my eyes. Filled the empty gorge

with the skyline   on my eyelid

We passed through medleys of sorrow, quick
as a trail of trees   quiet songs in soft light

Esther said she's sleeping better, falling in love
She's telling me, it's okay to live too much

                    love too much, as it's never
too much

We occupied the spaces between the carriages
          filled them up with old truth, heavy heart
ran along the length of that running, warm vessel
               stopped to grasp rusting mullions
with our dry fingers.

Our long hair, wind-braided, whipping
our loud faces in speed
                    we waited, together
to surrender
to the gradual ebbing
               of the old sea

So much passed   in the twilight of youth.

that that

was the year   love poured nothing back.

you learnt to pine, in silence, watched

the eagle and the raven fight the sun, chase it

into dusk—

to long, then, what was it?   all that doesn't belong to you,

                                                            accepts all of you

soaks in your warmth, drinks with an open throat, tilted jaw,

vomits a river of adulation into your eyes

          Love, you learnt, was divine discontent.

round and round fate will turn,

in being brutalised, we become brutal in return

Wisdom is going back to the places
you know best and know forever—
in the bookstore, you're drowning
in the vanilla scent of books, still yellowing.

A cat has fallen asleep on its face: a deep, unstirring
serenity catches you unawares.

A storm warbles beyond the window   whistling at you—
look out, in its heart you see a lone thing:
a dark head   in the wind, turning.

∞

I Hear Father is Dead in Another Country

One is as old as the days they remember.
Some make us age quicker, better.

Some slow in pace: something between a wish
and a prayer, something that is both. Say hope.

Light sweeping the white sand, across the cool,
quiet sea. Here, his consoling hand on my face—
on the brow, reaching, touching, brown, low.

The sound of a breath follows me here,
to a world ebbing in the cormorant's lair. He will
never now come to comb my hair, to save me

from the wrong affairs. There, the long shroud
falls from the sky, drops on his corpse, makes
its way to the pyre. Loud ash

from other burning bodies
flying in my sister's hair. Somewhere unknown
among the birds, one might find his verse.

A black hearse roots in my bones,
on a continent far, too far from home.

Palm fronds rustle. My eyes close.
My tousled head is made of clouds.

What Lives: Origin Story

In rooms gone black with memory, mother
  & father took turns to tell sister and I
stories to sleep: they had no heart for fiction,
& we no time
   to let the marrow of our little minds
stay warm. Hardening over winds
    that snored through cold bluebells
we foaled.

Cutting through hot loam, my ancestors arrived—
   whittled forest down to village, blew them
open into kingdoms; voices shrieked
   through war and brick, phylogenesis
of chest & tooth against history, banks loosened
   by rain.

Words turning back, voices
murmuring through dark into day.

I buried a carelessness in the pith
  of my orange heart. Inheritance
from that godless ancestor who picked
cherries   under sunlight & my feral appetite
for love? Sleeping with a thousand Penelopes,
he carved   a silver bed for them, etched
and honed. As he lay dying of syphilis, his mad
children   threw the bed away
    flinging their shame with it,
into the slow mouth of the sea.
  'and then?', I'd said to my mother.

How did Lillith's vanity spring in my chest?
   Music of sky snaking inside
the earth's flowers, in mucous & womb
as I firmed   into life. *Bodies leave bodies behind*
ma intoned, the mind unkinks from fiber and sinew,
   & now the daily ache, distending
the brain.

'Self-love, is also love of the other,
despite oneself'—my skin had absorbed it all,
    as she endured the protracted sorrow
of gestation. I carry this vanity
    I still conflate with self-love.
It's not mine, belongs to a cherubic
ancestor,   once furiously worshipped
in adjacent villages. A sage, a saint,
  who feared little   & found   after years
        of penance, his prayer was to undo the sins
of the kings that bore me, their past
shot through with blood
    loot, and rape   that the gods dined
with the sage already; they lay in his bed, clung
    to his jowl as water when he bathed,
trickled down his back, in the thin air
  he breathed; hot sun pickling
his dimpled arms   the Gods thronging
        among his people, filling the space
left by the things & souls
he cast out; deified under temple-eaves,
sightless & meditative, he towered—
venturesome   pilgrims trudging
from Kashmir, whirling
    through the Ganges, and arriving,
slow   for a glimpse, as they parted
with answers the holy route
prescribed. My great-grandfather
still sitting still
    within the clatter of feet,
pattering rain
the red noise of crowd and cattle.
How do I inherit this torrential anger,
    which really is fear
hiding my embarrassment, unkinking
    from these provincial ties?
We remember without language:

a woman ravaged in the family
she married into,
five   generations before mine.
This was the sin that begged this penance—

Fifteen year old widow cornered, left
    with her womb full the morning
after; when they knew her belly
    was proof of their crime, she was taken
to the woods, & left to die.
    This story trickles down
the mother lines
in whispers,
       whispers.

How do we forge these nameless trajectories?
Who chose to stay in the village?
  Who came to the city?
    Who was flayed alive?
     Who were the executioners?
The landowners? The code-keepers?

Who came to the capital? Who was brought
    against their will? Who,
was left behind?
Listen—
I know   the obsession with ancestry
these days but I'm afraid   to learn I have
    some whiteness muddying me,
that that unnameable thing
    done to a woman, was done then too
to her who could have been fifty,
    but was fifteen.

Where the will to surrender persists,
    history takes root—my grandfather
in the gulf a generation after, rescuing Indians
& Pakistanis, Kuwait against Saddam's wild war,

grandfather smiling in a silver print,
     smiling through tanks in the desert's liquid light.

We, here with my grandfather
who too is to tell stories in the dark, I'm
no longer a child, and he is about to die.

It was said that the soldiers grabbed
    all their eyes could. Ripped the stone
 clean from the flooring. Tiled
    marble at banks and hospitals
now cracking
into craters: what Kuwait was soon
          to be. They tossed out infants,
yesterday's leftovers, wrested them
    from their incubators,
the sanatoriums overflowed
    with the wailing of widows,
 the sins of demolition men.

My grandfather, they say,
    could have died with the babies
he tried to rescue in the Gulf,
   smuggle them home.
 Ninety, weary, his eyes now
   wander about the hanging lychees
run over details as he fixes his wristwatch,
   or cycles in the mornings through the orchards—
his eyes full of quiet, eyes that wished
once to be blinded, eyes now   that blink
and blink, and say nothing.

Gravedigger

All you have is a vague picture
   of a broken demigod, carrying
shovel over shoulder
   to the Qabristan—
you've remembered how
   the winter went, as it went on.
It was years ago, all your family
   young and alive in a slow,
warm taxi, and below, the sludge
   of overflowing drains
caked on the street—
an inert spectacle: a head like Jupiter
   in fine woven lace, a fly
in your memory's eye. What is
   a gravedigger's life
to his woman and offspring?
   Not a doctor. Pressingly required
only post factum.

      Not a hearse to his name, what
   has he to give them? What
is it to love him? Chief-Executive-
   General-Factotum.

 In this life, you could not
   tell Sisyphus from Atlas, glory
and shame shining in turns
   on the side of a coin against sharp light.
 Their backs are tired all the same.
Bearing both of their curses, our man
   donned a spade into the afterlife,
To make matters worse,
   he was born a muslim.
He plots his way onward
   to the wet earth, grass
shooting through green flesh.
   To meet whom?

Perhaps an old lover in the ground.
Man, woman, little ever known—
he sighs, says out loud
Allah hu! Better, never
to be found.

Daddy

Who was it that said, he loves like a tyrant,
yet within him, all anarchy and lawlessness?
That's what I had read, the day I heard you died.

I thought of the time you flung things around in anger,
I thought my light was spent early on, though I was just becoming.
First, I'd thought I would become my mother, yet

I look like you. I have your gaze. I have your hands. I have your rage.
Now you're gone, and I have no enemy. I am just like you.

Afterbody

This isn't about your clothes
        can't be a long robe. 'Leger', I hear the word
and feel a strange lightness coming on—I plucked
silver and grey feathers   your proud plumage
from the bowels of the almirah; interiors
        redolent with turpentine, ageing wood, swinging
mahogany doors wafting the family scent.
I opened them, long arms of diaphanous light
voyaged through years of your youth to mine;
rent open my dry mouth—blind swarm of silver
fish cloaked in grief. I choked in grief, could have
fallen, grew faint as I removed
articles of clothing from the dark, which meant courting
relief. Relief, for I breathed and knew I breathed. You were there
and weren't. From your afterbody I began, restlessly, to pluck
out   shirts   cufflinks   silk and linen
handkerchiefs   peacoats   cravats
bundies and hats;   kurtas   jackets a parka
old lockets (for a slender neckline—
you weren't always fat) shards of starched cloth, old
rags marking days when I walked into the house, my footprints
in the blood you'd retched. Now encrusted, sanguine.
        Pied stains turn ruddy on cotton (blood
        does not change colour on silk). Father, first
man, now a scent I can't bear. How did you leave
        this fight unfinished? Who were I to be against
in the absence of your madness? All this decadent solitude!
        Look, I know death is not what I smell,
death are the dead   that don't.

The Triptych

Inferno–Dante's quiet address.

Ciacco:
To find a familiar as though one were a witch
    making their way through violent, energetic dimensions
to see all suffer in the dark marshes, tell me, is he still your enemy
    or friend, against the equalizing torque of death, of afterdeath?—
In my suffering, he suffers as I, does he still
    in that black world, need
his lesson?
    Ciacco, who predicts the victory of tyrants
within three hot suns; did he not once
    dream of love? Do the wicked not
also dream of love?

Francesca:
Francesca, dearest, the things they accuse you of!
    Jealousy, lust, incest, vanity, fie to all!
Your sin was none but to forsake the myths
    of your fathers, it was wanting life
to be all your own, you were the hero
    seeking absolution, in your own private hell. Desire
does that for us: sets us free. And love?
    It makes in us,
something of the pure.

O, Francesca, would you have taken
    this poor pilgrim and seen your face in his?
If I found you before Paolo. If I held you in my eyes. You
    have done this before. Do it again. Soft as a dove, I come.
Be vain, I implore you. Beatrice
    can wait.

Cerberus:
Three mouthed fiend, forever
    famished. What do I do but cry for
the pain you endure, and what
    do I do, but see into your sixth eye, find your soul
...and there it is: a cracked reflection
    of the holy trinity.

Purgatorio–voices Dante hears.

What one would give to be loved in the way that they love. Always
the same tragedy: romantics left to suffer the basic, pragmatic. I see
you, Dante. Even in your dreams you're dreaming of her. So remote is
she. Yet your spirit never tires of the same hallucination. Balancing
will against destiny on this strange shore your might grows weary, but
you know it not. (Is she so different from any shade here?)

'Halt!' a voice goes. It is time for concert. Casella begins to chant,
croon. He must ease the pain of your living soul. Hear of the Exodus,
damned Princess. You who enslaved and on earth, wrung all life out.
"I sing" he moans "so you return to grace." So you know rapture, and
yet "...must I always humiliate myself, contending against heavenly
song ...playing eternal, and open on that wide, heavenly slope?"

Dante, it is God we always return to, and only for a moment we
find ourselves seduced by the beauteous. I warn you, hear this tale:
Belacqua, ignorant of his affliction, with apatheia looming over his
changing fate, even he, Pilgrim, has come to marvel at your shadow.
Such is beauty's grasp here. Wishful, distant. Manfred and his sheep,
an undulating thousand burn within, appear as a soapy oceantide of
outcastes. With the same song, they wait. I helm this world, though
Cato may believe otherwise. I do it for you.

Must we begin again, to begin again? Dante. Listen:
lightly,
        ascend.

Paradiso–Dante speaks.

On this cool, wrinkled soil, I step in with tired feet
    into that remote, geometric infinity of a new world.
My mind goes blank, I'm dreaming with eyes open. Aflame
    then cool, like a weapon, I'm being forged
in Haephestus' chamber. Look at this ruffled creature:
    a mountain no less, from foot to peak.
It once barked at me, and all about the nature
    of sin. All about
its proximity to love. Only earthly, though.
    My chest has in it a premonition, some sense
of how it all becomes heavenly, no matter how earthly.
    How do I know? I surmise it all.
By my ear, there is a flowing mouth:
    aglow, and tethered to the light within Virgil's frame.
He emboldens my fatiguing will, renews it
    …as though love were all but that.
Have we come so far, poet, only
    to come so far? To be left alone,
again? By the fourteenth trial, with my hand in Virgil's
    I was blinded by the flaring power of a million splendours
heavy upon my irises, and after, by the twenty eighth,
    I recast my gaze over my comrade. This time, with an unfamiliar
tenderness. As though it were Him. Is God, finally,
    a poet? Weaving the Word into the world.
Or is she a pilgrim? Casting life
    all around, where'er there is night.
The kernel of all that makes us good,
    is a speckle defeating the dark. It follows
us that hold on to our goodness: and we that let it
    not be disturbed by the deficient, or the perverse
by the cowardly or meek - these conditional modes of love.
    I guard this goodness in me. It's not mine to ruin.
It belongs to Beatrice.
    Goodness is knowing
we all pass among the passing
    as things and beings pass all
and another, always.

It was noon at the previous gate.
I was ready for the stars.
    At the Seventh Light,
now, a line becoming a circle,
    slow, becomes a line.

Bodies

We are not our bodies
we are the places we place
them, we are uneasy, bellicose, we
are seized; we are how we are
placed and chased within plots
of chance, of circumstance—
we are close, but never enough.

Crematorium

At Nigambodh Ghat, who is waiting for death?
Why am I so at ease here? Where death is mere
detail, no more event.

I hear a god in the smoke mind the forge.
Hear the large, wheezing echoes sound out
in the electric crematorium. A movement

that extinguishes bodies, loosens the ghost.
One, two, three, oar—Charon opening the door.

Look, now, here, a throat
gulping down hope—was it a dream, Langston?
Did it implode?

Viscera: Blood Fragments

I.

Wind flattening the slim, cool wood by night—
they arrive at day, men sprung from ancient soil.
   In hordes like buffaloes, shirtless, marching on—
a stampede irons out civilization; the sun shines through
genocide and fire. They pluck the charcoal and emerald
mess for its best, trunk and bark thrown back
against muscle and bruise; shoulder by shoulder, brown carcasses
carted to the atelier, serenaded all the way to their lorries.
You'd think such craftsmen have hearts thumping against
      their backs, from within; that they could shiny up a hull, well shaved,
carved to a definite stop. You'd think of Caillbeotte's floor scrapers, men
         without faces, without worry. Listen, they glisten
with sweat, with dignity. Throwing a nude arm, arm of wood,
then another into the shaver, cutter. Pile on pile become door and table, door
by door, they fit, so exquisite in homes of the future—now a row of houses lining
         a sunlit street. Watch water rub rock to boulder, time cook wood
to coal. Families sutured into homes, and day comes again—
a loose entrance frame swings slowly on its hinges. Something is born
between all that is known and not, when in its rasp, you feel
your head going quiet in the light, waiting for a train.

II.

A toothless body drops to a point as it falls through the mouth of a volcano
into the centre of the earth—a depth coughing amber, bone, sea. Time softening
human faces to ceramic, ash—forgiveness has lifted a veil to the thing
you now call 'an uncertain grief', everything disappearing and you, left praying
in the safe house of anger. The grooves of memory distract you, every now and
then—

Early aughts, Bengali market, the sun slathered our faces with fire. Just us there,
sister and sister, recalling our standard order a decade ago. Where it all went.
Somnolent breeze, clack and claver of childhood, outings with parents.
Well, ma anyway. Father always interested in conversations with others,
anything but us or what was ours. In a time gone: pink sun
reddening ma's hair, her breath quickening with love—"mera beta!"—

yet other words measured with caution. We were all a bit afraid of my father.
The routine cooing of a toddler nearby, now a cry. In a moment, a flickering
tenderness

settling on my sister's face. What was real and unannounced
as she extended her arms to arrest a small body in momentum, falling
quicker than we begin to notice. The crack of a little skull about to interrupt
the afternoon—a goddess, a messiah, a witch in catching, carrying
him lets a boy grow into a brooding man: what women do.
History, biology, evolution, civilisation—who we are
is present in the first impulse. All in the forward jerk
of a hand as it grips the nervous gaze of a child
mid mischief, mid euphoria.

III.

You learnt the word eviscerate when you first glanced
human viscera. A man lay dying but not all dead outside
          the hospital, Christ bled on the wall, as the man's arm
convulsed and swung off the stretcher like a rope over a well.
          A head wet with blood bisected by nature's knife.
Brains and bilge flowered on,
          a body near-docked by the shore for Charon.
Contretemps at a construction site, a phrase you saw
          at the back of your mind—"haemic disaster", words
sloped downward, dripped crimson and doctors
          with their all seeing eye, medical and weary
seemed to have only one way to see what I saw—
          "we were told such cases mattered little",
they had declared couples dead before, lodged them
          as injuries by suicide in reports, when it was well
and clear that a village had conspired to hang
          the two off a tree—these strange fruits of the east.
Ours are not the shores of Ilium, love is not
          free. Turning to us now, the doctor asked
"Do you send an entire dwelling to the gallows
          for the death of two?" by which he meant
a good citizen can't always be good, or true.
          So let the grief of a devastated conscience
turn them into Christ,
          so let them suffer, so let them die.

IV.

A poet once heard his own blood
singing in its prison, I'm so unlike him.

Exhume my heart, it exhales effluvia—
cut me open, I smell like Asia.

In the face of another's rage it's best
to offer a drink of water, be well reasoned.

Reinstate that old phrase: *a bloody catastrophe!*
Not 'treason.' Night after night, dreams

tuned to madness are corralled into a file—
think of the dream where you carried a dying
cossack on your back into the Indian sun, drew
the winter out of his bones: holding Dostoevski

warmed his blood, made it your own.
How do you love men that are dead and gone?

Keats' silken letters in the crook of your arm
Faiz is flitting by, a book under his arm.

(But, Medha, a book? for whom?)
Seeing glimpses of their faces in the faces

of alien men and, for that, wanting to marry
all of them. Never telling one about the other.

Turning one, then another, into father,
mother, and brother. All this while

being the other.

V.

A man stood outside my door in the white summer
barking the words 'donation drive!', as heat flooded the house
warming the marble floor. Rosebud afternoon blotting out
a lingering thought at the back of my skull. I stood in the building,
a building stood in me, sinking into a lull. A cow's tail in the distance,
brushed the flies off its rump. I was home alone. *Rakt!* He ejaculated.
Rakt daan! He clarified.

A donation of blood. He was really just begging, brewing,
riven by time. One can't donate something in urgent need—
someone always does need blood, you drew. Whoever thought
it venial to allow strange men to knock on women's doors, asking
them for the very and one thing that is still their own (No, not even time),
to call upon our conscience when least expected
in Delhi's infernal bunker. I slipped on a garment, the needle now
splitting my skin; I, unraveling; my blood coming loose.

VI.

The world zipping itself up, a sky
   made of ice, the ground
beneath your feet turns
   into water.
Thales points to the nature of things
   body, mind, vegetable, flower, all
sluice into water. A leopard is born
   in the Savannah, a cathedral crumbles
down in a sinner's dream.
    A woman lights a candle
on the mantle, prepares
   for a seance.
A writer notices all good poems
   & stories bear sunlight; his room
bright and silent, littered with paper. A crow
   perches on the back of a cow
grazing among the plastics
   behind a temple, an empty nest
is brushed by a breeze on a deodar
   branch. Dew turns to honey by the kiss
of an old God. A row of gulmohar trees
   made of quartz line a street in Delhi.
A man, a woman, in five minutes
   they will hold hands for the first time.
A boy's family has gone to work,
   he closes the window against a storm.
A tribal group in the forest, dancing
   when no one looks, fire, night. A year passes, has
passed, then another, then more
   all at once, now folding into a triangle
now becoming a napkin.
    Cattle and kine huddle
together, a quiet village
   goes about its day.

VII.

Who was that man scavenging
        for orange peels in the trash?
I waited for him before the school bus
        some mornings, when I didn't
        miss it.

I stood watching women
        who looked through him, men

gathering their children away
        from the mad fool. *This guy,*
        I thought, *saw a hole in the fabric*
and none quite believed him.
        What obsession

does to a man is well known,
        shunned; Dr. Physics here, they said

was a 'good professor', 'family man',
        'handsome too' (by a certain standard)

Undone by love and science, what
        did he learn, peering through the rip?

No coincidence that insanity
        and *insaniyat*
        are phonetically close.

VIII.

The destruction of art is also art, the sun
combs the earth's gardens and sister thinks
it's too much, *too much* light is not the 'right kind.'
My newest friend, a yogini, is sure to release her vivid
mind like an arrow to the point of true knowing—
it is Raza's bindu, or Husain's half made horses,
carrying me from dream to dream, until one turns up
at my door. My mother's best friend lived
in Canada, she trained horses for the Olympics,
sending them to me from an afterlife. In dreams
she is galloping into the distance, her hair
trailing auburn as she hurtles away to a point in the dark.
I think of her wrists, beads of sweat gathering
around them. I think of my mother, hunched over
her writing desk, mother who wept
when she read in a letter that auntie F had ridden
her way over to the other side. I draw a wrist I imagine
was hers and never finish the hand—
cacography, an old typewriter given to mother
by her father, now on my table, still in use for all this.
The first letter I ever loved: from aunt Francesca
who lived in Montreal, her horses near her still.
Years ago, there was the year of no internet and night
long tempests when mother's family gathered—
Four brothers, two sisters, lying on wet sand
against the torque of the ocean, kids strewn across
a land rich with oil and no war yet. Ma yet unknown
to the house about to wear her curtains next.

Δ

Acknowledgements

I'd like to thank the editors of the following journals for giving my poems the space and care they did:

Almost Island, Bad Lilies, Berfrois, The Bangalore Review, The Bombay Literary Magazine, Bangalore, Cordite Review, Coldnoon, Count Every Breath (Hawakal Books), The Dark Horse, Divining Dante (Recent Work Press), From Arthur's Seat (University of Edinburgh), Guftgu, Hakara, Hotel, Interpret, Indian Quarterly, Irish Pages, Kitaab, Outcrop, Poetry at Sangam, Stag Hill (University of Surrey), Still Point (King's College, London) and 3:AM.

Thanks

Thanks are owed to my mentor Don Paterson, my teachers Alan Gillis, Patrick James Errington and Miriam Gamble. To my classmates Amy, Liam-Lucille, Olivia, Tamara, Shelby, Heather and Han.

To the labour of Adil Jussawalla, Rohan Chhetri, Bharat Iyer, Ranjit Hoskote, Sandra Simmonds, Arun Sagar, Aishwarya Iyer, Alvin Pang, Tim-Tim Cheng, Niall Campbell, James Appleby, Rob Mackenzie, Gregory Leadbetter, Kathryn Gray, Andrew Neilson, Gerry Cambridge, Jim Carruthers, Samuel Tongue, Diarmid Sullivan, Patrick McGuinness, Priya Sarukkai Chhabria, Arjun Rajendran, Uttaran Das Gupta, Souradeep Roy, Haig Lucas, Ryan Van Winkle, Sampurna Chattarji, Nia Davies, David Bleiman, Anita Govan, Hadley James-Hoyle, Tobias Freeman, Benjamin Morley, Patrick Romero McCafferty in various capacities—for their crucial comments on the manuscript, for housing my poems in their journals and magazines, for sticking my shivering bones in front of a stable microphone, for the odd drink and chat in times of trouble and celebration all the same; finally, for being patient with all that goes into the making of a book.

Thanks to Calliope Michael and Russell Bennetts.

Thanks are owed to friends for their infinite love and warmth, for saying and doing things that helped me potter on: Jared Brill, Luka Smyth, Hannes Schumacher, Kenji Tsuchiya, Jess Martinez, Ruchika Joshi, Rajluckshmi Upadhyaya, Patrick Le Disez, Shomi Gupta, Shashank Bhatnagar, Gandharv Dewan.

Another set of thanks to the Behrens and Smyth families for welcoming me so kindly into Edinburgh and letting me stay in their lovely house on Pentland Terrace, where the large part of *Afterbody* was written.

Deep and profuse thanks to Divya Singh, my talented sister, who generously gave me the perfect painting for the cover of Afterbody and to my mother, Savita Singh, without whom nothing is possible. To my father, whose death has softened me.

Thanks, of course, to my partner Benjamin, for showing me the world.

Notes

p.18 **The Meadows:** The Meadows is a swathe of green between Marchmont, Tollcross, and the University of Edinburgh

p.19 **Painting Our Time:** line 5, Amazonia: The major forest fires surrounding COVID and Jair Bolsonaro's comments in the media concerning continued deforestation.
line 16/17: The Indian army attacking schools full of Muslim children. An 8 year old Muslim girl was gang raped by Hindu priests in a temple on her way to school. Newspapers showed the mother grief-stricken over a set of the girl's clothes. Her name was Asifa. The Indian army kicks in all doors to houses it deems pose a terrorist threat, most of which happen to be working class Muslim families.
line 24: 'The Sea' here refers to the Indian Ocean
section 2, line 7: Sahastradhara is a rocky patch in Madhya Pradesh, the largest state in India
section 3 line 4: a 'Dalit' is usually a neutral designation for a member of the lower rung in the Indian caste hierarchy. They have been derisively called 'untouchables' in the past. The Dalits are among the most discriminated members of Indian society. Suicides by students who belong to this section of the Indian population have increased over the years in educational institutions, owing to psychological and emotional abuse caused by student and teacher bodies. This poem was about a student called Rohith Vemula who described the problem in his suicide letter.
section 6: This is in reference to the epidemic of farmer suicides caused by land grabs and increasing rates of interest levied by rich Indian money lenders and land owners from upper caste families. Land grabs are also a common instance in the disputed territory of Indian occupied Kashmir.

p.25 **Rewilding:** 'heavy sad' is used by John Berryman in *Dream Songs*.

p.29 **Delhi, Day:** Southward: This means south of the capital. The southernmost tip of India touches the equator where it meets the sea. The shorelines are in peril due to the effects of climate change all along the entire Western coastline.

Northward: Contains many architectural remnants, preserved to varying degrees, from Indo-Saracenic times.

p.37 Aerie: Vignettes, Delhi
movement 1, p. 34: 'river' here refers to the Yamuna which runs through Delhi

p.40 This was an autonomous poem formally called 'a game of cricket'

pp.43-45 The Farmers' Protest: Men marched across the country barefoot in unprecedented numbers to protest the three farm acts instituted by the Government of India in 2020. This is the largest popular protest ever staged in human history with an approximated 250,000 people on the ground.

p.54 Utnapishtim: The boatman from the epic of Gilgamesh

p.57 The Radcliffe line: the line of control which separates India and Pakistan

p.58 translation from Hindi is 'line. shadow. body. end.'

p.65 Reference to Divya Singh's exhibition with Shrine Empire gallery, named 'Notes for Tomorrow'

p.74 Gravedigger: This poem was written in memory of Delhi's famous gravedigger Allah Hu. Qabristan is a name for a Muslim burial ground.

p.84 Crematorium: Nigambodh Ghat - a word for a Hindu cremation ground

p.85 Viscera: Blood Fragments:
p.86 'Mera Beta': Hindi for 'my child'

p.87 This is in reference to honour killings. Couples who dare marry outside the caste system are met with public hangings. These honour killings are meant to serve as an example for those who betray the prevailing code of endogamy. Often fathers are complicit with the village in the murder of their daughters.

p.88 'a poet' here refers to Mexican Nobel laureate Octavio Paz

p.89 'Rakt' means blood; 'Raktdaan' means a donation of blood

p.92 Yogini: a female practitioner of the materialist Yogic tradition. Raza, Husain: two prominent painters from the Indian Modernist painting tradition.

Medha Singh is a poet from Delhi, based in Edinburgh. She is a winner of the New Writers Award 2023 (Scottish Book Trust). Her work of translation *I Will Bring My Time: Love Letters from S.H. Raza* was published in 2020 through The Raza Foundation, in collaboration with Art Vadehra. Her poems appear in Irish Pages, Almost Island, 3:AM, The Dark Horse, Bad Lilies, Interpret, The Bombay Literary Magazine, Indian Quarterly, The Robert Graves Review among numerous others. Her work has been anthologized in *Singing in the Dark* (Penguin, 2020), *The Gollancz Book of South Asian Science Fiction* (Hachette, 2021), *Contemporary Indian Poetry by Younger Indians* (Sahitya Akademi, 2020), Best Indian Poetry 2018 (RLFPA editions), *Divining Dante* (Recent Work Press, 2021), *Future Library: Contemporary Indian Writing* (Red Hen Press, 2022); *Converse: Contemporary English Poetry by Indians* (Penguin Random House, 2022); *The Best Asian Poetry* (Kitaab, 2022).

Medha was longlisted for the Toto Funds the Arts Awards (India) in 2019 and 2020. She took her MSc in Creative Writing from the University of Edinburgh. Her work has been translated into Hindi, Spanish and French. She is editor-at-large at Pen and Anvil Press, Boston.